D1700482

# AN UNDERWATER GUIDE TO
# THE SOUTH CHINA SEA

© **Times Editions Pte Ltd 1992**

Published by
Times Editions
an imprint of Times Editions Pte Ltd
Times Centre, 1 New Industrial Road
Singapore 1953
Telex: 37908 EDTIME  Fax: 2854871

Printed in Singapore

ISBN 981-204-201-6

# AN UNDERWATER GUIDE TO
# THE SOUTH CHINA SEA

*Chou Loke Ming*
*and*
*Porfirio M. Alino*

TIMES EDITIONS

# Contents

**Foreword**
7

**The South China Sea**
9

**Marine Habitats**
13

**Coral Reefs**
17

**Competition and Cooperation**
21

**Conservation**
25

**Marine Life**
29

**Species**
39

**Index**
142

**Suggested Readings**
144

# Foreword

The unique geographical position of the South China Sea and the configuration of surrounding landmasses together with the variation in seafloor characteristics, has enabled it to contain many different types of marine habitats as well as support a remarkably high diversity of marine species. The South China Sea plays an important role in the economies of the countries associated with it, and its natural resources, both living and non-living, are rapidly being exploited by man whose populations in the region are heavily concentrated along the coasts.

However, the sea still holds vast areas which remain unexplored. It has a lot to offer in terms of its rich marine life, which needs to be appreciated and will be a shame to ignore. These living resources are the major contributors to marine tourism which is gaining importance as increasing numbers of people are attracted to admire life in a completely different environment. No two similar types of habitats are identical as geographical variation will influence differences between them. This makes the South China Sea all the more interesting. The sea continues to hold many mysteries which need to be understood. Its genetic resources are immense and this potential has not even begun to be tapped to serve mankind. It is of paramount importance that concerted efforts be taken to protect the marine habitats and their teeming marine life. Marine parks and reserves have been declared in many of the countries sharing this sea which points to a growing concern for its protection.

In preparing this book, the authors would like to record their deepest appreciation to the many friends who contributed the use of their photographs, so that a glimpse of the sea's fascinating marine life can be presented. They are duly acknowledged in the list of photo credits. The authors are also thankful to the Reef Ecology Study Team (National University of Singapore), and to the Marine Science Institute (University of the Philippines), for the valuable support and advice given throughout the preparation of the book. Special thanks go to Ms Grace Lim Su Yeong of the Reef Ecology Study Team, and Ms Reza Maria P. Khoa of the Marine Science Institute for their invaluable assistance with the organizing of the colour slides.

*Abundant fish life contributes effectively to the visual splendour of coral reefs which abound in the South China Sea.*

*Chou Loke Ming*
*Porfirio M. Alino*

# The South China Sea

With a total area of 3,400,000 square kilometres the South China Sea represents the largest body of water in an archipelagic region situated between the Pacific and the Indian oceans, and between the continental landmasses of Asia and Australia. This warm tropical sea itself extends from the equator north to almost the Tropic of Cancer, and across from Peninsular Malaysia to the Philippines. It is bordered by the continental Asian landmass along its western and northern flanks and the island masses of Indonesia and the Philippines along the southern and eastern flanks. A sizeable part of the sea extends into the Gulf of Thailand.

The seas of this region together with the South China Sea can be regarded as a geographical unit distinct from the Pacific and the Indian oceans. The bottom topography of the South China Sea exhibits an interesting variety of features such as the shallow continental Sunda shelf of 100 metres depth which dominates its southern half, and deep basins of 5,000 metres located in the northern sector. Small islands and coral reefs dot the sea.

Monsoonal climate has a strong influence on the South China Sea. The northeast monsoon between December and February, and the southwest monsoon between June and August change the surface current circulation patterns of the sea with predictable regularity. Wind forces are small but constant, while storms and typhoons are confined to the northern and northeastern sector.

Surface water temperature is affected by the monsoons. During the northeast monsoon when colder water masses from the higher latitudes flow into the sea, the surface temperature ranges between 26° and 27°C. Higher temperatures of 29° to 30°C are reached during the southwest monsoon. The annual variation in surface temperature is larger in the higher latitudes than nearer the equator. Salinity is maintained at around 33 to 34 parts per thousand but the nearshore waters usually have lower salinities of around 29 parts per thousand because of freshwater runoff from land, particularly during the rainy seasons.

The warmer surface waters, together with freshwater influence, lead to the lowered density of the upper layers. Because air temperature remains high and constant throughout the year, there can be no lowering of the temperature in the surface layers, unlike in temperate regions, which would then increase in density and sink. When this occurs, the bottom layers will rise to the surface, bringing along with them nutrients that are

*On undisturbed reefs, fishes like the grouper* **Epinephalus tukula,** *grow to large sizes. Many such reefs are still present in the South China Sea.*

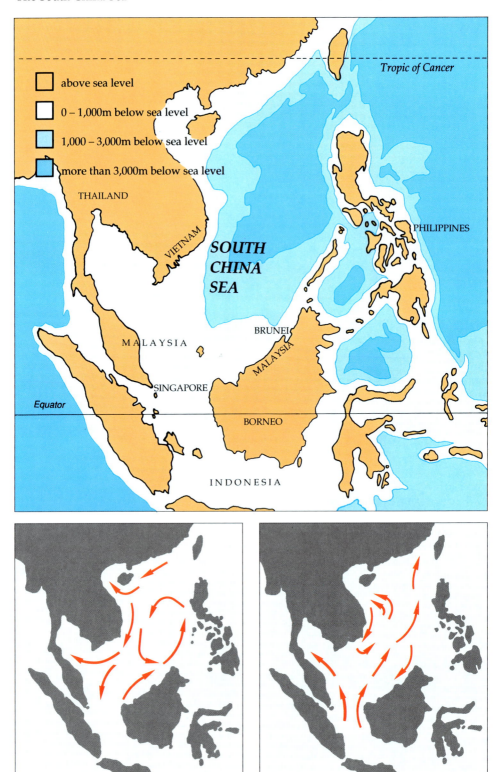

The tropical conditions of the South China Sea help to promote marine life. Sponges growing along a steep drop-off can reach remarkable sizes.

trapped at the bottom. This annual turnover of the water column is not possible in tropical conditions. The deeper colder waters remain trapped at the bottom together with nutrients that have sunk to the seafloor. This condition is observed for the greater depths of the sea. For most of the Sunda shelf, however, the entire water column remains fairly well mixed without much evidence of thermal stratification. The trapped nutrients at the bottom of the deeper regions of the sea, together with the cold bottom layers of water, can be brought to the surface in places where upwelling occurs. This happens in places where strong bottom currents flowing against a landmass sweep upwards to the surface, or where strong winds move surface waters away from land.

The South China Sea receives a continuous input of nutrients from the surrounding landmasses and large river outflows which contribute to its high primary productivity which is further maintained by the effective circulation patterns.

A variety of marine habitats can be found in the South China Sea. The interaction of all the different features enables the sea to support a rich marine life. A distinct characteristic is the high species diversity that can be found in this broad expanse of sea. All the habitats within it are marked by large numbers of species which make the South China Sea extremely interesting for the observation of underwater life.

*Opposite top: The South China Sea is surrounded by the continental landmass of Asia and the archipelagos of Indonesia and the Philippines. Sea floor depths vary greatly.*
*Opposite bottom left: Surface current patterns of the South China Sea during the Northeast monsoon (December-February).*
*Opposite bottom right: Surface current patterns of the South China Sea during the Southwest monsoon (June-August).*

# Marine Habitats

Flying over the waters of the South China Sea, the eye detects changing patterns of coasts and islands, land and sea. Through the sensors of a satellite or through a diver's mask, successive approximations of reality are conjured to describe these patterns which are the living habitats.

Following the yearly images from infrared aerial photographs, it is easy to notice decreasing strips of attractive reddish hues which indicate mangrove forests. Eternal white beaches meet the sea while some black basalt rocky shores melt into it. The shore continues into the shallow sea either as a sand, mud or reef flat. The gradient of the shore profile varies considerably depending on thousands of years of geomorphological changes. These are some of the buffer zones between land and sea where the fiddler crab plays its silent lovesong, and the ghostcrab runs frantically on tiptoes. The lumbering coconut crab finds solace in its craggy hole. While these areas provide shelter to such crabs, they also serve as nesting grounds of the long distance swimming green turtle or the high flying frigate bird. As the green turtle labours back to the sea, it may swim past seagrass beds. Also referred to as turtlegrass, they form extensive

*The coral reef flat forms an interesting marine habitat. Its plants and animals have adapted to fluctuating conditions of the changing tides.*

"meadows" on many of the backreef areas, but only in very inaccessible areas can rare herds of the sea cows, *Dugong dugon*, be seen to forage.

Further out the reef flat, the seagrass bed thins to reveal more coral heads. Dominance of the coral community builds up seaward to reach a peak on the reef crest and reef slope, where it is accompanied by myriad assemblages of reef fishes and other reef associated life. Coastal habitats offer harsh conditions to the organisms living there. Wave action and periodic exposure forces species to adapt, but at the same time these habitats receive a continuous supply of nutrients washed down from the land, enhancing growth of marine plants which in turn provides an abundant source of food to marine animals. These habitats are thus highly productive and do support a large biodiversity.

One soon realizes that these habitats actually form a complex continuum, linked primarily by the influence of tides and other events. Many organisms take good advantage of this linkage. For example, the rabbitfish *(Siganus)* spawns in the mangrove and seagrass areas, and its eggs float out to sea to develop into juveniles. They then return in large schools to the coral reef. Community changes also occur as populations interact. When a reef gets devastated by the crown-of-

13

*Seabirds like these boobies, **Sula sula**, establish rookeries on some isolated coral cays. It is not yet clear as to what extent they contribute to the integrity of the marine ecosystem but they definitely have a large daily diet of fish. Human encroachment into these breeding areas threaten the waterfowl populations.*

thorns starfish, for example, there is an accompanying change in the fish assemblage which registers a decrease in butterflyfishes and an increase in herbivorous damselfishes.

Across the sea's horizon, frigate birds dive in for their meal of anchovies which school away from the reef edges of atolls. This is a telltale sign of yellowfin tuna deeper beneath. A feeding frenzy develops as the tuna speed in on the anchovies, sometimes attracting the solitary shark. In these open waters, fast swimming fishes reign supreme, capable of travelling long distances at will.

The food chain begins near the surface with phytoplankton receiving adequate sunlight for their photosynthetic activity which transform nutrients into food. Sunlight penetration diminishes with increasing depth and at more than 200 metres, the watery environment becomes pitch black and cold. Still, certain forms of marine life exist under such unfavourable conditions of the deep, mysterious and unique in form and function, yet well-adapted to these factors.

The underwater world is constantly swept by silent movement of the water masses. Its sheer volume provides a greater space resource to its inhabitants, compared to the terrestrial environment. Environmental factors vary accordingly with depth, offering a variety of optimal conditions to suit different groups of marine life.

*Opposite top: Algal beds grow profusely in shallow intertidal areas when certain conditions are available. They make favourable habitats to a large variety of other marine animals.*
*Opposite bottom: Mangrove forests are important coastal buffers which help to stabilize sediment and prevent coastal erosion.*

# Coral Reefs

The coral reef is one of the highest biodiversity habitats within the marine environment. The dense concentration of colourful marine life makes it visually stimulating. Coral reefs are essentially massive deposits of limestone produced mainly by hard (or stony) corals. They grow well in clear, warm, shallow waters. The single-celled algae known as zooxanthellae which corals harbour in their tissues require adequate sunlight for photosynthesis, a process which aids the coral host in depositing its calcium carbonate skeleton more efficiently and to benefit from the nutrients generated in the process. A reef easily supports more than 3,000 different species of organisms. Effective nutrient cycling takes place between the species of the reef community so that the high production of nutrients is quickly taken up and almost completely retained within the ecosystem.

Highly interesting, the ecosystem is occupied by a multitude of resident species as well as visiting or migrating species. The latter include those which stay temporarily, using the reef as a nursery or feeding area. The wide variation in growth forms of corals and other sessile organisms

*Corals provide important relief to a reef and, in so doing, offer shelter and space to fish and other reef invertebrates.*

provide an important relief to the substrata, increasing space and shelter to other inhabitants, as well as surface area for settlement and growth.

Three types of reefs can be found in the South China Sea. Fringing reefs extend directly from the shore of a landmass. Such reefs are common around islands or coastal areas of continental landmasses. Patch reefs are associated with raised seafloors and the tops are usually not exposed except temporarily at very low tides. Atolls are circular in shape with a central protected lagoon. They often develop from submerged volcanoes and are usually found in the deep open sea. The seaward slopes, plunging steeply down to the ocean depths, support living communities that are different to those in the shallow lagoon.

In their ecological role as natural breakwaters, coral reefs play an important part in buffering the forceful impact of waves against beaches and thus protect them against erosion. They are important natural laboratories for education and scientific research, particularly in the search for biologically active chemicals. The habitat provides a source of food for man as it supports concentrated populations of exploitable species. They are also valuable as a resource for recreation and tourism. Man has been exploiting coral reefs without

*The diversity of coral reef life together with the variety in shape and form of the inhabitants create interesting underwater landscapes.*

giving much thought as to how they can be sustained over the long term. Reefs have been ravaged to provide building and construction materials, and plundered off much of the food-important species as well as the ornamentally-valuable species.

The destruction by man is usually irreversible in extent. The once rich life-giving ecosystem gets reduced to a pathetic mass of rubble devoid of life and colour. Even damage by natural influences like typhoons and the crown-of-thorns starfish is never to the extent of preventing suitable recovery. The South China Sea supports many fringing and patch reefs nearer the landmasses and atolls in the open sea. Many of the reefs which are easily accessible are rapidly being degraded by man, but pristine reefs in the remoter areas which have not yet been subjected to man's

impact are present, demonstrating nature in its full glory and splendour.

However, many of these outlying reefs have become the subject of multinational territorial claims by countries surrounding the South China Sea. The Spratly Islands with their pristine reefs are being claimed by more than five countries, not so much for the beauty of their coral reefs as for the suspected presence of large exploitable reserves of oil and gas. Not for long, these reefs can remain inescapable from man's long reach.

Like a desert oasis, a coral reef is an immensely biologically-rich eco-system. It represents high-density living of a vast array of marine species. Without coral reefs, the variety and concentration of marine life will be significantly reduced.

*Opposite: The height of this sponge makes it a favourite of the featherstar **Himerometra** to exploit the water column for the supply of food brought along by the sea current.*

# Competition and Cooperation

From the tranquil depths of the coral reef, one can hear the crashing of the waves against the shallow reef crest above. In this conflicting seascape, the diverse inhabitants constantly engage in tiny battles or useful alliances. These are just some of the biological interactions which have been referred to as competition and predation, symbiosis and coevolved relationships. The ultimate reasons as to why such phenomena exist have always intrigued man. Coral reefs of the South China Sea are excellent arenas for these processes. The opportunity to observe these wonders of the underwater world can reveal more of nature's mysteries.

Why are there competitive interactions and their various processes? These interactions occur when common or similar resources are being utilized by individuals of the same or of different species. An important resource which is usually competed for is space. For sessile organisms especially, space is critical for settlement or shelter. The seemingly immobile corals are good examples of the variety of such manoeuvres. In their competition for space, they can interfere with the growth of their neighbours either directly or

indirectly. They have stinging cells known as "nematocysts" which can be used against a neighbour growing too close. Some corals such as *Galaxea*, have long sweeper tentacles armed with nematocysts which can reach out and kill the neighbour. Corals can also digest living tissues of near-by colonies by extruding highly modified filaments from their bodies. Soft corals are known to exude toxic substances against their neighbours so that they can have more space to accommodate their growth in size. Also, since most reef corals are dependent on light, the faster-growing species can block sunlight from reaching their neighbours, causing them to eventually die.

There are other non-direct interference modes that organisms employ in their life history strategies (such as fecundity, recruitment, growth rate and mortality) which contribute to their success in establishment within the community. A continuous spectrum of a mixture of these traits can be observed, from those organisms which have high fecundity, high recruitment, fast growth but high mortality, to those which have low fecundity, low recruitment, slow growth but low mortality.

Aside from competition and physical influences such as storms, light, depth and substratum quality, predation can affect the composition of

*Competition for space on reefs is constantly contested by many organisms. Opportunistic species are quick to colonize any available space, only to be forced out later by aggressive species.*

21

*Some invertebrates like this purple sponge exude toxic chemicals to kill and overgrow this live hard coral colony,* **Leptoria phrygia.**

underwater communities. One extreme example is the population outbreaks of the crown-of-thorns starfish, *Acanthaster planci*, which can efficiently diminish live coral cover of reefs with devastating effect. Grazing pressure from herbivores can also be considerable in areas where there is an abundance of algae either as blooms or as monospecific stands such as those in seaweed farms.

In the underwater world, shape and colour adaptations can facilitate the inhabitants in their feeding behaviour, which includes territorial recognition and agonistic displays. Colour patterns are important for fish, particularly in clearer shallow reefs. Nudibranchs exhibit an array of bright colour schemes. Why is this so when they have no shells to protect their soft bodies? Because it is important for their survival to warn predators that they are highly unpalatable. Nudibranchs feed mainly on sponges or soft corals which are chemically toxic or distasteful.

If organisms cannot warn potential enemies with bright colouration, then they resort to shields, united front alliances or establishing a common market with other species. These can be seen in many classic symbiotic relationships such as: corals with symbiotic algae in their tissues, corals with small shrimps and crabs amongst their branches, the cleaner wrasse and other fish species, the clownfish and the sea anemone, the hermit crab and the sea anemone.

*Opposite top: The pagurid hermit crab acts as a chariot to its hitchhiker, the sea anemone* **Adamsia**. *At the same time, the anemone provides protection to its carrier host through its array of stinging cells.*
*Opposite bottom: In the never-ending competition for space in the reef environment, various strategies are employed. The horny coral,* **Briareum stechei**, *puts out elongated sweeper tentacles to kill the edges of the encroaching hard coral.*

# Conservation

For most island nations, the sea has always been the giver of life. While coastal margins remain in a constant dynamic state of flux, storms and typhoons often make dramatic changes to these natural processes. Around the South China Sea, dependence on marine resources has resulted in their heavy exploitation with very few attempts made at understanding the implications involved. The high densities of the coastal populations in the region have contributed to the discordant pressures on marine resources. Over 50 per cent of the populations' protein intake comes from the sea, and a large but undetermined portion of the workforce is dependent on the marine environment. This dependence comes from various forms of resource utilization such as fisheries, marine transportation, offshore exploration and mining of mineral and non-mineral reserves, as well as other indirect support services.

The beauty of the sea has also elicited from many of us a passionate love for it. Marine tourism has become an important concern in the economies of these countries, with beach resorts and the provision of diving facilities occupying a consid-

erable proportion of the industry. When considering what the sea can offer, the challenge put forth is in deciding whether these potentially conflicting uses are warranted, and if so, whether they can be made on a sustainable basis.

A review of the various users will show that aside from the seemingly positive gains from the utilization of marine resources and habitats, most of these activities have negative impacts which are manifested in the irreversible depletion of resources or degradations of habitats. The fisheries industry is now faced with declining average annual catches. Many fishermen are forced to resort to more efficient techniques and to venture out further to new fishing grounds. The more desperate ones use illegal and often hazardous fishing methods such as blastfishing and cyanide poisoning. Not only are stocks being diminished, but habitats are also being degraded, particularly by increased sedimentation resulting from land development.

The tremendous pressures on the sea require immediate action and strategic planning in order to ensure long term sustainability of its living resources. Obviously, strong enforcement measures have to be implemented and supported by the necessary legal support structures. This is where research becomes

*A large multispecies concentration of the mushroom coral, **Fungia**. Unlike all other hard corals, the mushroom coral is solitary and remains unattached to the substratum during the adult stage, making it a favourite for collectors.*

25

important as it will provide essential information that will form the required basis for the formulation of an effective management plan. Aside from research, regulatory activities have been started either through community-based management of declared marine parks and reserves, or through various multi-use protected area systems. Alternatives aimed at reducing total dependence on natural stocks such as mariculture, sea ranching and artificial reefs are also helpful.

*Left: Artificial reefs are now serving to shift pressures away from natural reefs, but the solution really lies in effective management of living coastal resources.*

*Below: Fish forms a very important source of protein to the coastal communities of the South China Sea.*

*Opposite top: Studies by marine biologists indicate that a large proportion of the South China Sea's coral reefs have been degraded.*

*Opposite bottom: Various efforts are being made to counter the depletion of some species due to over-exploitation. Culturing of endangered species like the giant clam, **Tridacna**, can help in restocking the reefs.*

# Marine Life

The high diversity of marine life in the South China Sea makes it impossible to represent them fully in this book. Almost all the major groups of marine plants and animals can be found. Their form, structure, colour and behaviour never fail to attract the attention of the recreational diver or the serious marine biologist. The sea still holds many secrets and reveals them very slowly to the most interested of observers. The beauty and grace of its inhabitants, however, are freely available for the admiration and enjoyment of anyone who appreciates nature in this watery world.

## Algae

Better known as seaweeds, these simple non-flowering plants are without roots or leaves. They are attached to the substratum by a holdfast from which a stem-like "thallus" arises, itself being either branched or unbranched and in some species bearing leaf-shaped fronds. In structure they range from small uncomplicated filaments to large bushy growths. Seaweeds are divided into four categories depending on the main photosynthetic pigments present in

them, and are popularly referred to as green, blue-green, red or brown algae. Many species in the region are harvested for food and are either collected from the wild or cultured on reef flats. As plants, they are considered to be important primary producers contributing significantly to the lower levels of food chains. Growth is encouraged by sunlight because of their ability to photosynthesize, and further enhanced by increased nutrient levels of the waters. Areas closer to land-based runoff have a greater abundance of algae which compete with corals for settlement space. *Ulva* is a common green algae on such areas. The brown algae, *Sargassum*, is another widespread and fast-growing brown seaweed in the region, with distinct air-bladders that help to hold up the thick bushy growths in the water column. These branches break off during rough sea conditions of the monsoons and float away to new destinations. Red coralline algae produce calcium carbonate which helps to cement rubble and contribute towards reef building. The green alga, *Halimeda*, also participates in building reefs by incorporating calcium carbonate. Single-celled green algae known as zooxanthellae, live within the tissues of hard corals in a symbiotic relationship, which promotes their growth.

*A closer view of* **Cirrhipathes anguina** *shows the stalk coated by the tentacles of the non-retractable polyps. The resilient stalk is highly resistant to breaking.*

*The South China Sea supports a rich variety of underwater habitats, each with a high diversity of marine life that makes underwater observation extremely interesting.*

## Seagrasses

Unlike algae, seagrasses are true flowering plants that have evolved to flourish in shallow areas. They have an extensive root system which ramifies through the substratum and helps to consolidate loose particles of sand and silt. Leaf blades with venation patterns extend above the substratum together with seasonal flowering shoots. About one-third of the 50 species of seagrasses known throughout the world occur in the coastal habitats of the South China Sea. Like algae, they contribute towards the primary productivity of the habitat and form an important food source to numerous species of marine animals, including the sea cow *Dugong dugon*, and the green turtle *Chelonia mydas*. They play important ecological roles in providing food and shelter to numerous species and are used as nursery grounds by many of them.

## Sponges

These animals which belong to the phylum Porifera represent the lowest level of multicellular organization. They can be considered as aggregations of cells which are specialized for different functions but not organized into tissues or organs. These cells can be thought of as being organized around a series of water canals or chambers through which a one-way flow of water is maintained, bringing with it nutrients and oxygen. Sponges are sessile and come in an interesting variety of sizes, shapes and colours.

*Opposite: Jellyfishes, close relatives of corals, swim by pulsating their bell beneath which hang the mouth tentacles.* **Acrometoides purpureus** *is a common rhizostome jellyfish in the South China Sea.*

## Coelenterates

This is a very large and diverse group of marine invertebrates, representing a higher level of organization than the sponges, in that the specialized cells are grouped into organs and the animal has a definite shape. Jellyfishes, corals, hydroids, anemones, sea fans, etc. belong here. Although extremely variable in form, they all share a common basic body plan of a sac-like body around a gut where food, water, oxygen and wastes pass either in or out through a single entrance surrounded by tentacles which are armed with stinging cells known as nematocysts. While the jellyfishes and some stages in the life cycle of hydroids are free swimming, many of the other forms are sessile throughout their adult phase.

## Flatworms

Marine flatworms are often flamboyant and appear to glide over uneven substratum with great ease. When swimming, they are among the most graceful of all swimming animals. They have thin, delicate bodies which enable them to hide under rocks or in narrow crevices.

## Segmented worms

The free-living forms are easily recognized by the segmented appearance of the elongated body. They usually burrow in the seafloor or seek shelter under rocks and in crevices. Some of them have numerous glass-like bristles which provide them protection from predators. The tube-dwelling worms are usually confined to the tubes which they themselves secrete for protection and the texture of which depends on the species. Some secrete a parchment-like tube which may be reinforced by sand grains or shell fragments. Others secrete a hard calcareous tube. For added protection, these tubes are embedded in the seafloor or in coral heads. Some tube dwelling worms have large showy feathery tentacles which are fully extended from the open end of the tube to trap food particles. These colourful tentacles are retracted with astonishing speed at the slightest hint of danger.

## Molluscs

Another major group of marine invertebrates, these are represented commonly by gastropods, bivalves and cephalopods. The soft body is protected externally by a calcareous shell, single in the case of gastropods (snails) or a pair in the case of bivalves (clams, oysters, mussels). In the opisthobranch gastropods, the shell is very much or totally reduced while in the cephalopods (octopuses, squids and cuttlefish), the shell lies within the body and serves a support function.

Gastropods move about the bottom in search of food. An enormous variation in diet and feeding mode is exhibited by them. The cone shells have a highly specialized feeding mechanism equipped with powerful toxins and harpoon-like teeth which can paralyze active prey such as fish within seconds. Some gastropods prey on other gastropods by boring a neat hole through the shell of the prey into which digestive juices are secreted.

Well known among the opisthobranch gastropods are the sea hares which still retain a vestigial shell, and the nudibranchs which have lost all trace of a shell. Nudibranchs are extremely colourful and some protect themselves by secreting an unpleasant and distasteful liquid.

Bivalves are usually filter feeders. They remain buried in the seafloor or are attached to rocks and submerged

*A head-on view of the tiger cowrie shows the mantle spread round over the shell's outer surface. This helps to give the shell a natural highly-polished lustre.*

man-made structures. Some lie on the seafloor and are capable of moving by extending a "hatchet" foot or by actively flapping their shell valves. Giant clams have zooxanthellae in their tissues just like the hard corals and derive the major part of their nutrition from this partnership.

The cephalopods together with some species of opisthobranchs can secrete a copious amount of dark, opaque liquid which acts as a smoke screen to confuse the enemy and make good their escape. To catch their prey, they depend very much on their muscular tentacles — eight in octopuses and ten in squids and cuttlefish — lined with suckers. Octopuses and some cuttlefish are able to change their body colouration instantaneously to match their surroundings so that they remain effectively camouflaged.

## Crustaceans

Crabs, lobsters, shrimps, barnacles and many small-sized species that make up the zooplankton community belong to this group which is related to insects, spiders and scorpions on land. These crustaceans are typified by an external skeleton which provides protection as well as support. Mobility is allowed by the many joints in the hard coating. In order not to restrict growth, this outer skeleton is shed periodically and replaced by a larger one to accommodate increase in size. During this process, while the new skeleton takes time to harden, the animal is most vulnerable to predators and must take refuge in crevices or under rocks.

Barnacles remain fixed in position throughout their adult life. They are abundant especially around the tidal level and settle heavily on many man-made structures in the sea including the hulls of boats and ships.

*The spiny lobster, **Panulirus ornatus**, which is commonly sought after by man, is a voracious predator. It hides most of the time during the day but hunts actively at night.*

Their protective shells enable them to withstand periods of exposure during ebb tide.

Crabs, lobsters and shrimps have as added protection, spines of various sizes on their external skeleton. The lobsters most commonly found in the South China Sea are the spiny lobsters which have beautifully patterned shells and small claws, unlike the strong oversized claws that their temperate cousins have. Crabs use their pair of claws to ward off enemies as well as to handle food. Some colourful crabs are poisonous, but many others, together with shrimps and lobsters, are commercially valuable as food.

## Echinoderms

This entirely marine group includes seastars, brittlestars, sea cucumbers, sea urchins and featherstars. The variation in form and structure is shared by a body plan based on a five-radial symmetry. This plan explains why most species of seastars and brittlestars have five arms or multiples of five. The body plan is secondarily over-ridden by a bilateral symmetry in sea cucumbers and some sea urchins.

Seastars feed on anything ranging from detritus to meat. Some carnivorous ones prey on bivalves and are efficient at pulling the shell valves apart with their arms. The crown-of-thorns starfish is also included here and is known to affect the coral reefs whenever they occur in large numbers. Brittlestars have arms which are more clearly demarcated from the central body disc. The arms are also flexible and serpentine, and more elongated.

Sea cucumbers are familiar forms on reef flats or on the seafloor where they feed on organic matter. Many are capable of defending themselves by secreting long sticky translucent threads and if handled further will eviscerate almost completely.

Sea urchins are well protected by their numerous spines and many species are commonly associated with coral reefs. Many of them feed on macroalgae while moving about actively over the reef and are known to cause damage to the reef.

Adding elegance to the underwater world are the featherstars. These colourful creatures have numerous long feathery arms which undulate gracefully with the sea currents to trap particles of food.

## Bryozoans

Not too well known are these small colonial animals which are each protected and bound together by a hard covering that can be encrusting or shaped into a delicate lattice structure. They are widespread and abundant and cannot be ignored.

## Tunicates

Sometimes referred to as sea-squirts, these animals represent the lowest form of vertebrate life because the free-swimming larval stage possesses a notochord which is a precursor to the backbone found in vertebrates. The adult tunicate is sessile and they are either solitary or colonial. The body wall can be tough and leathery in some species or thin and translucent in others.

*The transparent body wall of some species reveals clearly the internal structure of the tunicate. Most obvious are the transverse gill slits of the large pharynx which appears like a large basket.*

*The highly forked tails and strong body musculature of* **Carangoides** *make them powerful and extremely fast swimmers.*

## Fishes

Fishes dominate the entire water column in terms of abundance and species. These vertebrate animals are well-adapted to swim the seas and in so doing have the advantage of being able to exploit widely distributed resources. The freedom to swim long distances without being completely influenced by sea currents has contributed much to their success. Some are engineered to swim fast and depend essentially on speed to escape predators or successfully hunt prey. Others cannot swim fast but depend on manoeuvrability in order to escape. Among slow swimmers, many other protective mechanisms are employed. There are those which can puff up their bodies so that they become too large to swallow; there are those which have defensive spines which may or may not be connected to toxin glands; there are those which are effectively camouflaged or have bright warning colours; there are those with a tough armoured body; and there are those whose body shape enables them to weave in and out of narrow crevices and tight corners. Because of these adaptations, fishes exhibit an amazing variety of shape and form, from the typical streamlined fish shape to the elongated eel shape and other bizarre forms like the venomous stonefish, sea horse, porcupine fish and sole. Some are more sedentary than others. The lizardfish, anglerfish, scorpionfish and stonefish spend a lot of time resting on the bottom, while the pufferfish, sea horse, pipefish and lionfish prefer to remain motionless for periods of time in the water column. Among the fast swimmers, the flying fish stands as a unique example of a fish that can cover effective distances through the aerial environment. Its modified elongated pectoral fins and body musculature enable it to flap these fins and literally skim the air just above the sea's surface.

Also remarkable is the kaleidoscope of colours exhibited by fishes, particularly those associated with coral reefs. They enhance the visual impact of the underwater world and add the vibrancy that makes it all so attractive.

Two major groups of fishes are recognized, the cartilaginous fishes and the bony fishes. The first group has a skeleton that is largely composed of cartilage and includes the rays and the sharks. The skeleton of the second group is of bone and includes all the other known forms of fish.

Fishes of the South China Sea are being heavily exploited with the inshore areas showing signs of serious over-exploitation. They form the major protein source for the surrounding countries. Colourful reef fishes are also caught for the

aquarium trade, and the diversity of such fishes in this sea contributes to the intensity of this activity.

## Reptiles

Some of these air-breathing animals have returned to live in the sea and have modifications that make them suited to the marine environment. Sea snakes and turtles are two clear examples in which the adaptations are so efficient that they have difficulty moving about on land. Being air-breathers, they need to come to the surface now and then, but they have physiological adaptations that allow them to remain submerged for long periods with each breath of air. Sea snakes have their tails flattened sideways so that they function efficiently as oars. Turtles have their feet modified into flippers which enable them to swim extremely well. Like the fish, turtles of the South China Sea are heavily exploited, particularly their eggs which are laid in nesting holes on beaches, dug up and then covered by the females.

## Mammals

Like the reptiles, some of the air-breathing mammals have also created a niche in the underwater world for themselves. Whales, dolphins and porpoises have lost their hind limbs and the front limbs are modified into flippers. The tail moves in an up-down motion unlike the sideways movement seen in fish. Their respiratory physiology enables them to remain long underwater but they must surface for air. Dugongs are more commonly associated with the nearshore waters where they feed on seagrass.

*Epinephalus is a grouper which can be distinguished from Cephalopholis by the number of dorsal spines, 11 in the former and 9 in the latter.*

# Species

Marine plants ———— 40
Sponges ———— 42
Hard corals ———— 44
Soft corals ———— 52
Sea anemones ———— 56
Gorgonians ———— 58
Hydrozoans ———— 64
Jellyfishes ———— 66
Coral relatives ———— 68
Flatworms ———— 70
Segmented worms ———— 72
Bivalves ———— 74
Gastropods and Cephalopods ———— 78
Opisthobranchs ———— 82
Crustaceans ———— 88
Seastars ———— 92
Brittlestars ———— 96
Sea cucumbers ———— 98
Sea urchins ———— 102
Featherstars ———— 106
Tunicates ———— 108
Rays and sharks ———— 110
Eels ———— 112
Butterflyfishes ———— 114
Damselfishes ———— 118
Parrotfishes and wrasses ———— 120
Triggerfishes and surgeonfishes ———— 122
Serranids ———— 124
Snappers and grunts ———— 126
Pelagic fishes ———— 128
Venomous and poisonous fishes ———— 130
Other reef fishes ———— 132
Reptiles ———— 140

## Marine plants

*Marine plants play a critical role in the productivity of tropical seas. They can be divided into vascular and non-vascular plants. The former (such as seagrasses) have a distinct zonation especially in the South China Sea. The non-vascular plants are commonly known as algae or seaweeds and are categorized into four groups based on the predominant pigment — green, brown, red and blue-green.*

**1** – *Some species of the green alga,* **Caulerpa**, *are utilized as food by coastal inhabitants.*

**2** – **Valonia** *is a green alga with an unmistakable form. The entire globular structure is of one single cell.*

**3** – *The brown alga,* **Sargassum**, *grows thickly along the reef edge. Luxuriant growth is arrested by rough seas during the monsoons which causes them to break and drift with the currents, floating with the aid of small air-bladders.*

**4** – **Lithothamnion**, *a red coralline alga, contributes towards reef building through its ability to form calcium carbonate.*

1 ▲

2 ▲ 3 ▼

4

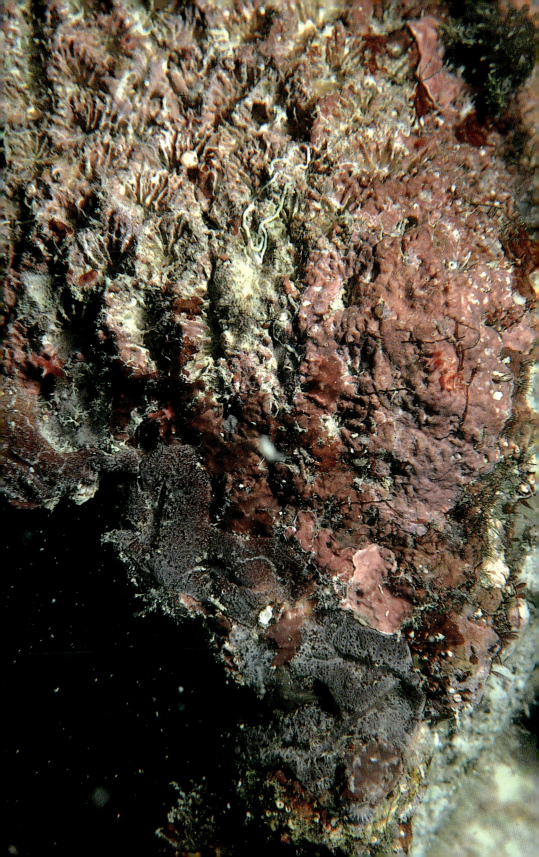

# Sponges

*Although representing the lowest level of multicellular organization, sponges occur in a variety of shapes and sizes, and are sometimes brightly coloured. They are common and play important roles on a reef, sometimes boring into hard corals or coating the weaker coral colonies.*

**5** – *A colony of the common bright blue sponge,* **Xestospongia***, growing on a hard coral colony, demonstrates their opportunistic colonization and growth.*

**6** – *Some sponges such as* **Clathrina** *have a growth pattern that forms a delicate lattice structure.*

**7** – *This bright yellow sponge adds further to the colourful environment of the reef. The outgoing water current leaves through the large openings.*

5 ▲ 6 ▼

7

## Hard corals

Hard corals form the framework of a reef through their calcium carbonate deposits. Most of the hard corals harbour single-celled algae (zooxanthellae) in their tissues and are known as hermatypic corals. Sunlight is important to their growth as its energy is required to power the photosynthetic process of the zooxanthellae. Hermatypic corals therefore thrive best in clear, shallow waters. The ahermatypic corals which do not have zooxanthellae can be found in low light conditions, but do not grow as fast as hermatypic corals.

8 – **Tubastrea aurea** is an ahermatypic coral found in low light conditions such as under ledges and in underwater caves.

9 – The unmistakable fleshy polyp of **Plerogyra sinuosa** are fully extended during the day, providing maximum exposure of coral tissue containing zooxanthellae. The slender tentacles which trap plankton are extended only at night.

10 – Another ahermatypic coral is **Dendrophyllia** which usually develops extensive branching.

8 ▲ 9 ▼

10

11 ▲

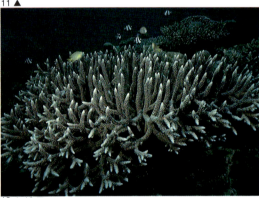

12 ▲ 13 ▼

**11** – *Fully extended polyps characterize the coral* **Goniopora**. *Being elongated, their efficiency in trapping food particles is increased. Clownfishes in the absence of sea anemone hosts sometimes use large* **Goniopora** *colonies as their hosts.*

**12** – *The branches of corals such as this colony of* **Acropora splendida** *offer shelter to some reef fishes. Seeking refuge within the branches, these fishes manoeuvre their way about making it difficult and usually impossible for larger predators to seize them.*

**13** – **Acropora** *dominated reefs are widely distributed throughout the South China Sea. The common tabletop* **Acropora hyacinthus** *is seen here with the longer branching* **Acropora nobilis** *above it. Most branching* **Acropora** *are fast growing and can colonize large areas quickly.*

**14** – *The reef habitat forces corals of different species to grow close to one another in order to utilize the tight space to full advantage. Here, a colony of* **Porites** *(above) grows next to a colourful colony of* **Acropora** *(below).*

14

15 ▲

16 ▲ 17 ▼

**15 – Pavona cactus** *are found in more sheltered parts of the reef, away from surf action, and has thin contorted plates which are delicate.*

**16 –** *The richly textured colonies of* **Pachyseris** *appear most of the time like interesting underwater sculptures. Large colonies make very arresting seascape.*

**17 – Pectinia alcicornis** *is a common inhabitant of lower reef slope zones, and are quite tolerant of low light conditions and heavy sedimentation.*

**18 –** *When fully extended, the finger-like tentacles of* **Turbinaria** *give the hard coral a soft appearance. Confusion is likely to arise with the brown algae of the same generic name.*

18

**19** – *The pretty and delicate* **Seriatopora hystrix** *is commonly seen on most reefs of the South China Sea. It is recognized by its tapering sharp tips and neatly arranged longitudinal rows of polyps along each branch. They thrive best in clear waters.*

**20** – *Corals like* **Mycedium elephantotus** *have a laminar growth form and are found in areas of a reef such as the lower reef slope which are not exposed to heavy surf action.*

**21** – *Long sinuous valleys and ridges characterize colonies of* **Symphyllia**, *a massive coral common on reefs of the South China Sea. Their resemblance to the mammalian brain gives them the common name "brain coral". Colonies can attain large sizes on established reefs.*

19 ▲ 20 ▼                                                    21

# Soft corals

Unlike hard corals, soft corals do not deposit a consolidated calcium carbonate skeleton but have dispersed calcareous sclerites within their tissues. They have a radial symmetry based on eight or multiples of eight instead of six as in hard corals.

**22 – Efflatounaria** has retractile tentacles and broods its eggs on the surface.

**23 –** The pink eggs of **Sarcophyton** are developed internally before being released for external fertilization.

**24 –** Very large colonies of **Sarcophyton** are not rare. They sometimes dominate a reef flat and give strong competition to the slower growing hard corals. The egg cowrie, **Ovula ovum**, is often associated with them.

22 ▲ 23 ▼

24

25 ▲

26 ▲ 27 ▼

**25** – *Like* **Sarcophyton**, **Lobophytum** *forms thick leathery colonies. They are differentiated by the variation of their lobulations and distribution of the polyps.*

**26** – *Some species, such as* **Parerythropodium fulvum fulvum** *brood their eggs (shown here in yellow) on the surfaces of the polyps.*

**27** – **Xenia** *is recognized by its large tentacles located on polyps which are non-retractile. The colony appears to pulsate as the individual tentacles open and close rhythmically.*

**28** – *Branching soft corals of the genus* **Dendronephthya** *stand out easily as the most striking of the group. They can contract into a small insignificant mass especially when currents are strong, and extend fully during slack currents for the individual tentacles to trap food from a larger volume of water.*

2

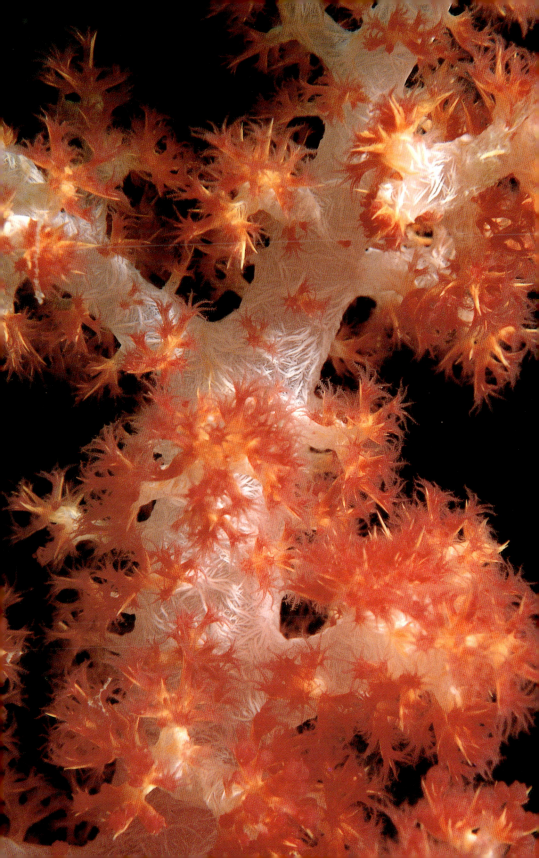

## Sea anemones

*Usually attached to the substratum by a disc-like structure, they can move to another location should conditions force them to. Some species burrow in the sand but with the tentacles exposed at the surface. The tentacles carry stinging cells which help to capture prey. Some species serve as host to clownfishes in an association which benefits both partners.*

**29** – *Often growing to large sizes particularly on undisturbed reefs, **Radianthus** adds motion to the reef through the swaying of the elongated tentacles in response to water currents.*

**30** – *Many of the sea anemones found on the reef such as **Stoichactis** belong to the family Stochactidae.*

**31** – *The brightly coloured body of this **Radianthus** species provides a great contrast to the drab brown tentacles.*

**32** – *Clownfishes (**Amphiprion ocellaris**) wriggle with much confidence among the tentacles of **Radianthus ritteri**, receiving effective protection from predators.*

29 ▲ 30 ▼

▲ 32 ▼

# Gorgonians

The gorgonians or sea fans, and sea whips, are generally bush- or fan-shaped, or a single elongated stalk. The skeleton is strengthened by a horny material which also allows flexibility, enabling large colonies to withstand strong currents and not to break from their holdfast which secures them to the substratum.

**33** – Gorgonians are often distinguished by their general growth form such as the elongated finger-like **Elisella**, as opposed to the other two forms illustrated, **Juncella** and **Melithaea**.

**34** – The simple whip-like **Juncella** grows well in deeper parts of the reef. Featherstars are commonly seen perched on them.

**35** – **Melithaea** forms a broad, highly branched fan, and is a favourite resting place with featherstars.

33 ▲ 34 ▼

35

**36 – Isis**, *also known as the bamboo coral and usually found in lagoonal back reef areas, has fleshy leathery tissues.*

**37 –** *One group which includes* **Acalcygorgia** *has no calcareous deposits in their skeleton and are characterized by non-retractile polyps. They also show interesting variations of form and colour.*

**38 –** *The branches of this* **Acalcygorgia** *form an ideal resting place for a featherstar whose arms blend well with the branches of the gorgonian.*

39 ▲

40 ▲ 41 ▼

**39** – *The beauty of* **Acalcygorgia** *is reflected again in this form where the whitish tentacles stand out vividly against the red stalks.*

**40** – **Euplexaura** *does not have well-defined walls around each polyp.*

**41** – **Ctenocella** *has a distinct lyre-like growth form and thrives well in deeper areas.*

**42** – *The fully extended soft tentacles of* **Solenocaulen** *contrast against the tough leathery branches of the colony. The hollow branch stalks serve as a shelter to many small crabs.*

42

43 ▲

## Hydrozoans

*The hydrozoans include small feathery hydroids, some of which resemble ferns, as well as coral-like colonies which secrete calcium carbonate like the hard corals. Most are noted for their strong stinging ability. They are also referred to as hydrocorals.*

**43 – Millepora**, *commonly referred to as the fire coral, can grow as branching colonies. Their stinging ability is well known, resulting in a sharp burning sensation.*

**44 –** *At times,* **Millepora** *forms large colonies like these extensive plate-like colonies of* **Millepora platyphylla** *growing close to tabletop* **Acropora**.

**45 –** *Branching colonies of* **Distichopora violacea** *are easily distinguished by their small size and colour which is pink or violet with white branch tips. They are common in darkened areas of the reef.*

**46 –** **Aglaophenia**, *another stinging hydroid, resembles ferns more than animals.*

44 ▲ 45 ▼

46

47 ▲

## Jellyfishes

*These pelagic animals swim with graceful rhythmic pulsations of a bell beneath which trail the tentacles. Although capable of such movements, they are generally carried along by water currents. The stinging cells along some of the tentacles enable the jellyfish to trap its prey. Some fish species which seek shelter among the tentacles do not appear bothered by the stinging cells.*

**47** – *Small fishes are commonly associated with the underhanging arms of jellyfishes.*

**48** – *The bell of the rhizostome jellyfish,* **Phyllorhiza punctata**, *is easily recognized by the numerous white spots. The eight mouth-arms hang as neat bunches beneath the bell ending in short compact filaments.*

**49** – **Acrometoides purpureus**, *a rhizostome jellyfish, has numerous tentacles trailing down between the arms.*

**50** – *The trailing arms of some jellyfishes can be very extensive, making them most formidable to prey and swimmers alike.*

48 ▲ 49 ▼

50

## Coral relatives

*Groups that are related to the corals and well represented in the South China Sea are the cerianthids and the black corals.*

**51** – *Cerianthids resemble sea anemones but have their muscular bodies encased in mucous tubes which are buried in the sand. Their long slender tentacles can be quickly withdrawn completely into the tube.*

**52** – *Black corals have two general growth forms, one of which is a long loosely-coiled stalk as seen in* **Cirrhipathes.**

**53** – *The other growth form of black corals is the branching tree type exhibited by* **Antipathes.**

**54** – *The branching structure of* **Antipathes** *provides much opportunity for featherstars to cling to, and contributes further to the underwater landscape.*

51 ▲   52 ▼

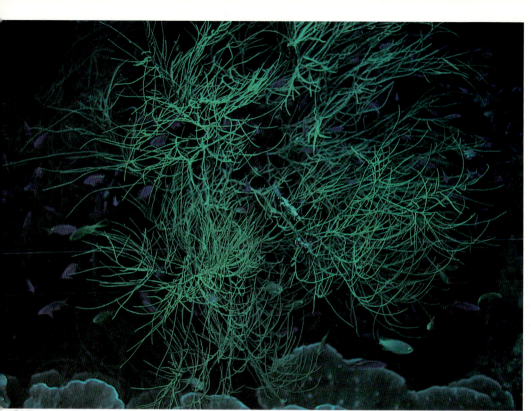

## Flatworms

*These free living worms are amazingly flat. They glide effortlessly over the roughest substratum and, when swept off, can swim by sending rhythmic waves down the sides of the body. Many are brightly coloured.*

**55** – *The deep pink* **Pseudoceros affinis** *glides over rocks in search of food. Most flatworms are considered to be carnivorous with small invertebrates forming the main diet.*

**56** – *Sending a rhythmic series of waves down its sides, this flatworm* **Pseudoceros** *swims daintily to a different location.*

**57** – **Thysanozoon flavomaculatum** *demonstrates the striking colour pattern that can be seen in many flatworms.*

55 ▲ 56 ▼                                                            57

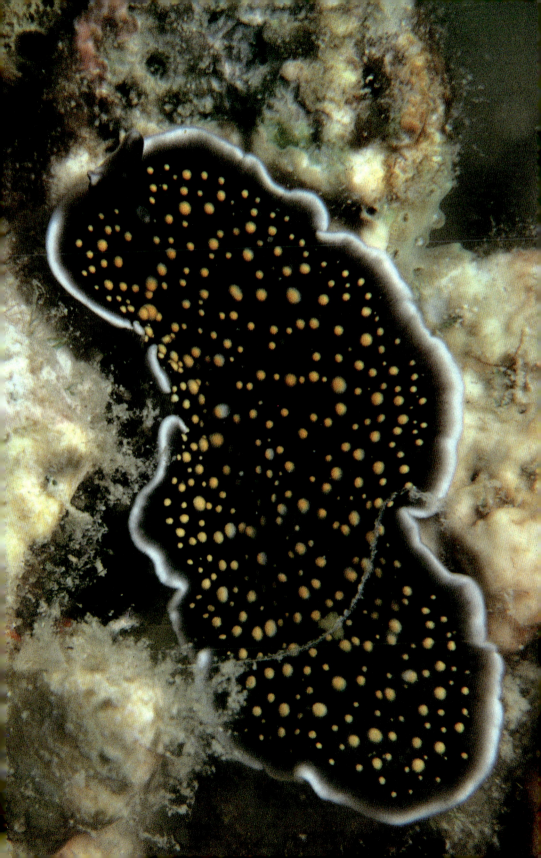

# Segmented worms

One group of segmented worms that confines itself within a tube obtains food with its large feathery tentacles that spread out like a net over a bigger area. This gives them the common name of fan worm. Their tubes are usually embedded in live coral, rock or the sandy bottom.

**58, 59** – Sabellid fan worms such as **Sabella-starte** with its more distinct double whorl of feeding tentacles, and **Sabella**, build tubes which are not calcareous but parchment-like and impregnated with sand or mud. They also prefer to build their tubes in live corals.

**60** – Some fan worms create their tubes in the sandy bottom and, with favourable conditions present, can carpet an area by their dense concentration.

**61** – The Christmas tree worm, **Spirobranchus giganteus**, is well known for its pinetree-shaped tentacles which come in a variety of bright colours. These serpulid worms build their calcareous tubes within live coral colonies such as **Porites** which they prefer.

58 ▲ 59 ▼

# Bivalves

*Although bivalves are basically equipped with a pair of shell valves which protect the soft body, there is a large variation in the size, shape and structure of the shell, as well as the mode of living.*

**62** – *In giant clams, the soft mantle fuses into a single piece of tissue spread between the shell valves, leaving one opening for the intake of water and another for exhalation.*

**63** – *Like all giant clams,* **Tridacna maxima** *can reach large sizes. The mantle tissue harbours zooxanthellae like in corals and is fully spread out in the day to receive sunlight.*

**64** – *The mantle of giant clams usually displays an interesting variety of patterns as well as bright colours.*

62 ▲ 63 ▼

64

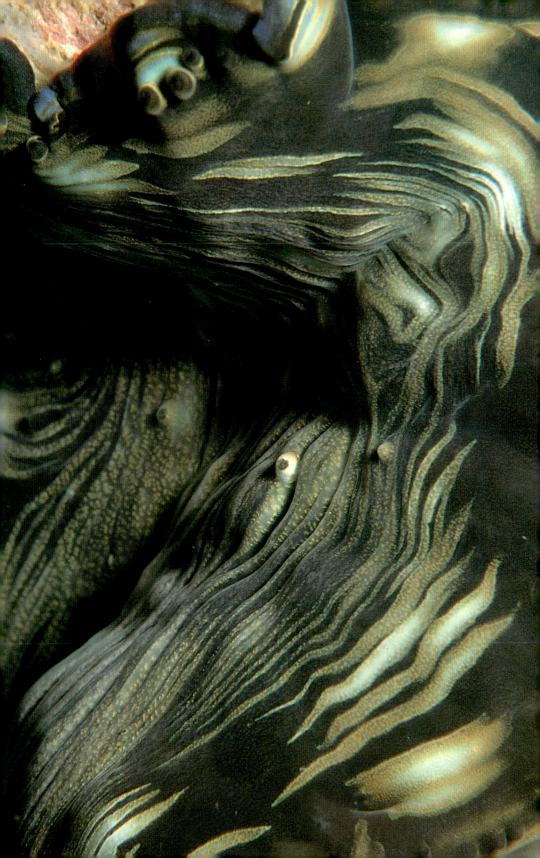

**65** – *This* **Pycnodonte** *bivalve is perfectly camouflaged when its valves are sealed tight. A slight separation of the valves reveals the zigzag outline which immediately exposes its presence.*

**66** – *The fan shell,* **Atrina***, embeds itself in the substratum, leaving the sharp edges of its shell valves exposed through which the distinctive mantle can be seen. On mud-sand intertidal flats, these protuding valves are hazardous to those walking barefooted. They are commonly sought after for food.*

**67** – **Pedum spondyloideum** *commonly embeds itself within the* **Porites** *coral where it remains well protected against its enemies. It enlarges the cavity in the coral as it grows by inhibiting coral growth around it.*

65 ▲ 66 ▼

67

# Gastropods and Cephalopods

68 ▲

69 ▲ 70 ▼

Gastropods form the largest and most diverse group among the molluscs. The single protective shell is coiled and into which the entire soft body can be withdrawn for effective protection. The muscular foot with which the animal crawls about is well developed.

**68** – Cone shells such as **Conus aulicus** are always sought after for their beautifully patterned shells. They are deadly predators with a highly specialized mode of feeding. They inject harpoon-shaped teeth into their victims, together with toxic venom, to paralyze their prey.

**69** – The tiger cowrie, **Cypraea tigris**, is among the largest of cowries and is commonly associated with coral colonies of tabletop **Acropora**.

**70** – The egg cowrie, **Ovula ovum**, has a jet black mantle that contrasts highly with the pure white shell. They are commonly associated with soft corals.

**71** – Another associate of the soft corals is the false cowrie, **Calpurnus verrucosa**, which has an attractive dotted mantle.

71

**72** – *Cephalopods have internal shells and can swim strongly by using the muscular body to create jet propulsion. They are efficient predators. Some species of the cuttlefish,* **Sepia***, breed in coral reef areas.*

**73** – *The triton shell,* **Charonia tritonis***, shown here in an inverted position with the body completely withdrawn into the shell and protected by the operculum, is a known predator of the dreaded crown-of-thorns starfish. They too have been exploited in great numbers by shell collectors.*

**74** – **Strombus** *has a long narrow operculum which it uses to dig into the ground and pull itself across in a leaping motion. This effective way of locomotion enables it to cover much ground.*

**75** – *The well-developed eyes of strombids are carried on the ends of stalks.*

72 ▲ 73 ▼

▲ 75 ▼

# Opisthobranchs

The shell in these molluscs show different stages of reduction. In many cases, the reduced shell is covered by the foot or the mantle. In the nudibranchs, the shell is completely lost and the animal has to resort to other means of protection. This usually takes the form of glands which secrete strong chemicals and the bright colours serve to warn predators to leave them alone.

**76** – The long, slender body of **Pteraeolidia semperi** characterizes the aeolid nudibranchs. Carried along the entire back of the body are elongated tentacles called cerata arranged in clusters.

**77** – **Flabellina** feeds mainly on hydroids in such a way that the stinging cells are not discharged but can be transported within the aeolid's body to be positioned along the surface of the cerata ready for use against its enemies.

**78** – In **Phyllodesmium**, the slightly flattened cerata are elongated and numerous, serving to shield the small body.

76 ▲ 77 ▼

78

79 ▲

80 ▲ 81▼

**79** – *The very common and widespread* **Casella atromarginata** *has a distinctive wavy black-bordered mantle edge.*

**80** – **Chromodoris** *is widespread in the tropics and has bright attractive colours. Species diversity is high. All of them have a pair of rhinophores which are specialized sense organs and a tuft of gills on the back.*

**81** – **Casella cincta** *has an arresting colour pattern that makes it stand out against the background.*

**82** – *Feeding mainly on hydroids,* **Flabellina rubrolineata** *protects itself using the stinging cells of its prey. Its bright colours serve to warn enemies to stay away.*

82

83 ▲

84 ▲ 85 ▼

**83, 86** – *The phyllidians have a characteristic body form with a leathery texture. The body is usually ornamented with ridges and a variety of protuberances. They are also brightly coloured as is seen in* **Phyllidia ocellata**, *with its distinct black rings, and* **Phyllidia varicosa**, *with its yellow protuberances. Both species are common on reefs of the South China Sea.*

**84** – **Chromodoris coi** *moving about and feeding on stinging hydroids, which it devours without any harm to itself.*

**85** – *Another interesting soft-bodied form is exhibited by* **Nembrotha**, *which feeds mainly on bryozoans.*

86

## Crustaceans

*While the external skeleton provides coral reef crustaceans with protection, many of them have interesting colour patterns which serve either as warning colouration or cryptic colouration. Some exhibit interesting techniques in effective camouflage.*

**87** – *The sponge crab,* **Dromia dormia**, *has modified pairs of legs with which it carries a sponge over its back all the time for effective concealment.*

**88** – *The hermit crabs make use of empty gastropod shells to protect their soft inner body. They carry the shell about as they go scavenging for food. Some of them position small anemones on the shell above their heads as an added protection against enemies.*

**89** – *The reef crab,* **Thalamita** , *is an active predator and hunts for prey usually at night. Its strong pincer-like claws can easily subdue most prey, and at the same time discourage enemies.*

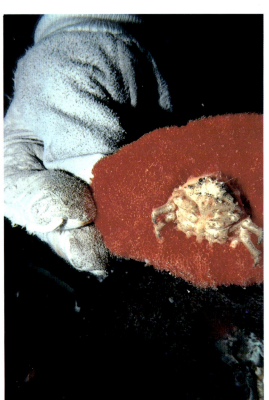

87 ▲ 88 ▼

89

**90** – *The crab,* **Macropipus***, preys on sessile invertebrates from which it derives the toxin that is used for its own protection.*

**91** – **Stenopus hispidus***, also known as the banded shrimp, usually occurs in pairs and are often found sheltering in crevices.*

**92, 93** – *Many reef-associated shrimps such as* **Periclimenes***, with a more transparent body, and* **Stenopus hispidus***, with extremely elongated pincer arms, get their nutrients from the mucus of corals. These shrimps are attractively coloured with many parts of the body completely translucent. Many of them are collected for the aquarium trade.*

90 ▲

91 ▲ 92 ▼

93 ▶

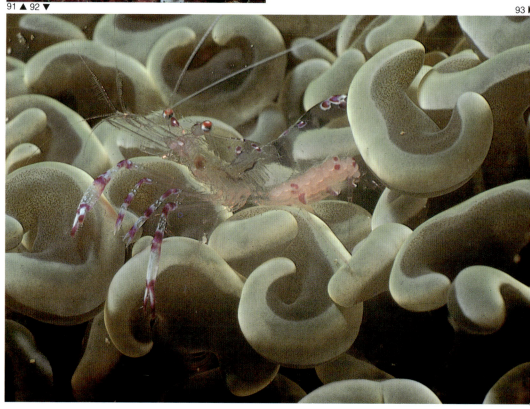

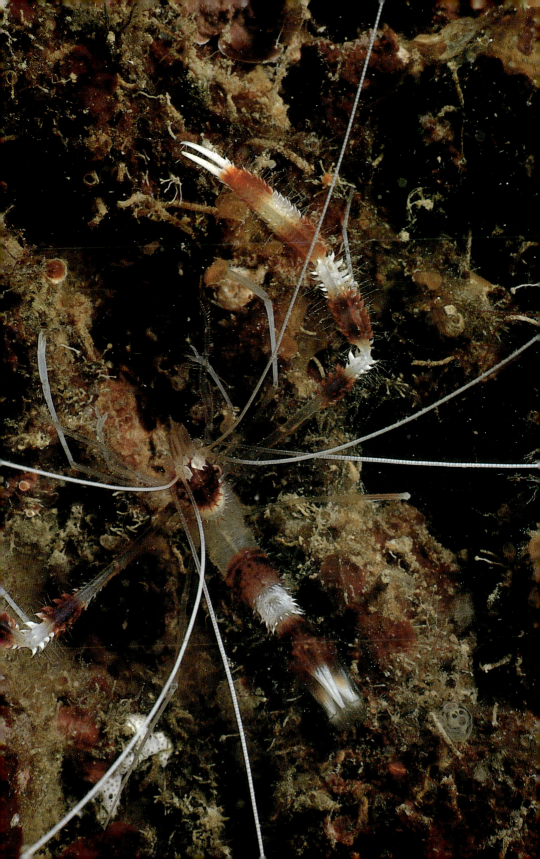

## Seastars

Seastars have a five-radial symmetry with most species exhibiting five arms although some may show departures from this. They are known for their high powers of regeneration and those which have lost an arm or two quickly grow new ones in place.

**94, 96** – The blue seastar, **Linckia laevigata**, is a common associate of coral reefs. Its distinct blue colouration makes it easily recognizable. Together with many other species of seastars, **Linckia laevigata** feed actively on bivalves (left). Using their numerous sucker-like tube feet on the bottom of their arms, they force open the bivalve and extrude their stomachs over the soft body parts of the prey.

**95** – Plague proportions of **Acanthaster planci** can easily devastate a reef within a short time. The reasons for their outbreaks are not clearly known and are the subject of intensive study.

94 ▲ 95 ▼                                                                                                    96

97 ▲

98 ▲ 99 ▼

**97** – *The body test of many seastars such as* **Choriaster granulatus** *reveals intricately sculptured patterns designed to provide rigidity and strength.*

**98** – *The cushion star,* **Culcita novaeguineae**, *loses its typical star shape as it grows into an adult. It is often seen feeding on coral tissue.*

**99** – *The crown-of-thorns seastar,* **Acanthaster planci**, *a voracious feeder of coral tissues, has more than 10 arms, all bearing sharp spines connected to venom glands.*

**100** – *This brightly coloured seastar,* **Fromia monilis**, *is seen here crawling over a faviid coral. It is easily one of the more beautiful seastars.*

100

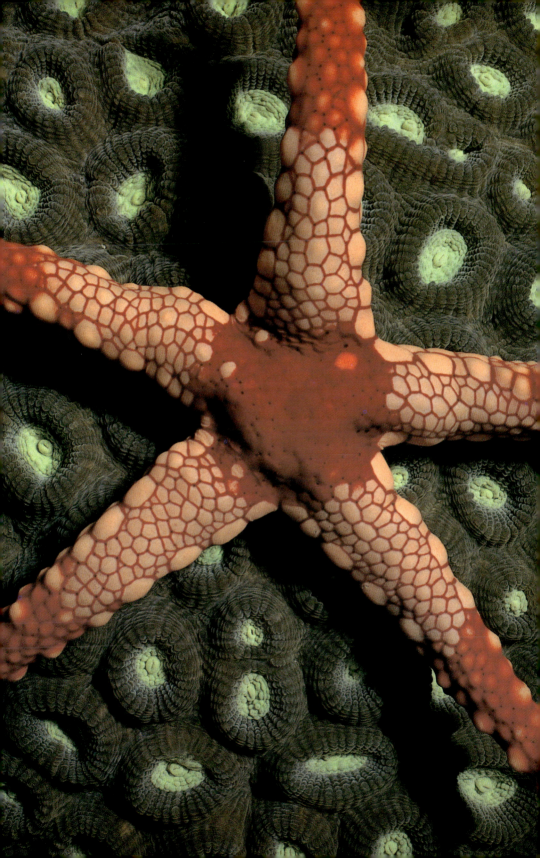

# Brittlestars

They can be distinguished from seastars by their arms which are more well-defined from the central body disc. These longer but thinner and more flexible arms enable them to move at remarkable speed. They usually hide in crevices during the day and in many cases, live in cavities within other living organisms such as sponges.

**101** – **Ophiomastix** uses its long serpentine arms to move about quickly on the reef. When caught by the arm, it will readily break off the trapped arm in order to escape.

**102** – A close-up view of the arm of **Ophiomastix** shows the high degree of flexibility throughout the entire length.

**103** – The clearly demarcated arms of **Ophiothrix** carry thin long needle-like spines for protection.

**104** – The pretty **Ophiolepis superba** has long arms which are more flexible along the vertical plane than the horizontal plane. The body plates are distinct.

101 ▲

102 ▲ 103 ▼

104

96

# Sea cucumbers

105 ▲

106 ▲ 107 ▼

Also known as holothurians, sea cucumbers have elongated bodies without any arms. The body wall which may be thick and leathery or thin and translucent, is strengthened by scattered skeletal plates or spicules.

**105** – *The synaptid holothurians like* **Synapta maculata** *have long thin-walled bodies which can be stretched out into a narrow tube. However, the body is very resistant to breaking.*

**106** – *A head-on view of* **Bohadschia graffei** *showing the bushy oral tentacles which are spread out in search of food.*

**107** – **Actinopyga lecanora** *has a fatter but shorter body. The thick leathery body wall bears interesting markings.*

**108** – *Species of* **Synapta** *can crawl through tight spaces because of their soft flexible bodies.*

108

109 ▲

110 ▲ 111 ▼

**109** – *The well-known* **Holothuria edulis**, *which is common on reefs and often gathered for food, has an unmistakable pink underside.*

**110** – **Stichopus chloronotus**, *a common sea cucumber on reef flats in the South China Sea, is easily distinguished by its colours.*

**111** – **Bohadschia argus** *is recognized by its unusual but beautiful body markings.*

**112** – **Phyllophorus**, *which is often found on algal beds, has the peculiar habit of compacting itself into a ball shape.*

112

# Sea urchins

113 ▲

114 ▲ 115 ▼

Sea urchins are immediately known by the presence of numerous spines all over the body. For many species, the spines are long and give the urchin almost impenetrable protection. Most of them hide in crevices during the day, and emerge at night to feed. They can move about quickly and cover much ground.

**113, 116 – Diadema setosum** is easily the most widespread and abundant sea urchin in the South China Sea. Large populations have been implicated as the cause of reef degradation in some areas. The young **Diadema setosum** (right) already has long spines and is well protected from predators.

**114**– The short cropped spines of **Toxopneustes pileolus** do not appear capable of providing much protection, but the urchin has small specialized scissor-like structures which can inflict wounds as well as inject strong toxins into the enemy. They are known to have caused human fatalities.

**115 – Heterocentrotus mammillatus** has uniquely thick, club-shaped spines.

116

**117** – *The small but attractive* **Echinometra mathaei** *has a distinct white collar around the base of each spine. They can bore cavities in coral rock where they fit in snugly for shelter.*

**118** – **Asthenosoma intermedium** *is the most strikingly coloured sea urchin. The spines bear different bright colours.*

**119** – *A closer view of* **Asthenosoma intermedium** *reveals the cluster arrangement of its spines.*

**120** – **Echinothrix calamaris** *bears spines of different sizes and colours. The finer spines between the thicker ones are the ones that provide ready protection.*

117 ▲ 118 ▼

## Featherstars

*Their many long feathery arms make them among the most graceful of all marine creatures. Although capable of moving about, they spend most of the time holding on to the substratum or to other sessile marine organisms, their favourites being sea fans and sea whips. With their long wavy arms, they are able to trap plankton and other food particles as the sea currents sweep by.*

**121, 123** – **Comanthus bennetti** *with its many arms, and the less bushy* **Comatula**, *are two examples which demonstrate the striking colours exhibited by featherstars.*

**122** – *The holdfast tentacles of* **Lamprometra** *allow it to cling on to a soft coral without being swept away by the current. However, if swept off, it can swim by undulating its many arms in a well-coordinated and fascinating rhythm.*

121 ▲ 122 ▼                                                         123 ▮

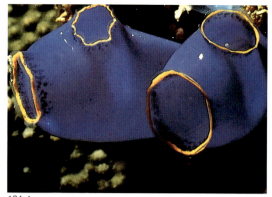

124 ▲

# Tunicates

*Also known as sea squirts or ascidians, they are closely related to the vertebrates. They have a body wall resembling a basket-like tunic. Water is drawn in through the inhalent siphon and discharged through the exhalent siphon. Food particles are filtered off from the continuous stream of water. Tunicates can be solitary or colonial.*

**124** – *The clavelinids are colonial forms which come in an array of colours such as the bright blue with distinct yellow margins seen in this species of* **Clavelina**.

**125** – *The solitary* **Polycarpa aurata** *has a thick leathery body wall which is coloured yellow with purple to violet markings.*

**126, 127** – *Colonial tunicates sometimes form dense mats of a single species or of mixed species.*

125 ▲ 126 ▼

127

## Rays and sharks

*These fishes have skeletons which are made of cartilage. The skin is rough with numerous denticles embedded in it. Fertilization is internal and the young are born alive or laid as eggs separately within capsules known as mermaid's purses. They have very well-developed sense of smell.*

**128** – *Commonly found resting under coral overhang is the bluespotted ray,* **Taeniura lymna**.

**129** – *The spotted eagle ray,* **Aetobatus narinari**, *with its characteristic white spots, is an agile and graceful swimmer.*

**130** – *The blunthead shark,* **Triaenodon obesus**, *is usually associated with coral reefs and often found resting on the floor of underwater caves and large crevices.*

**131** – *The white-tipped reef shark,* **Carcharhinus albimarginatus**, *common in the reefs of the South China Sea, rests beneath a ledge and shares the shelter with the soldierfish,* **Myripristis murdian**.

128 ▲ 129 ▼

# Eels

*These fishes resemble snakes with their elongated bodies. The soft dorsal and anal fins form a low continuous row down the body which includes the caudal fin. The body form makes them well adapted to hiding in crevices. With their sharp teeth, they can inflict a nasty wound. Attacks on divers have seldom been without provocation.*

**132, 133** – *Eels spend much of their time in crevices and dart out to capture passing prey. Their sharp teeth and strength enable them to deal effectively with active prey.*

**134** – *When swimming, eels like* **Gymnothorax** *throw their elongated bodies into a series of waves which propel them along.*

**135** – *A moray,* **Gymnothorax**, *cautiously eyes food offered by divers. Large morays have been described as dangerous and aggressive. Divers swimming by close to the eel's hiding place sometimes get bitten when the eel acts instinctively to defend its territory.*

132 ▲ 133 ▼

## Butterflyfishes

The butterflyfishes are closely associated with coral reefs and the highest number of species occurs in the South China Sea. They are distinguished by their bright colour patterns which may change between day and night.

**136** – *Usually found in the deeper parts of reefs, this millet-seed butterflyfish,* **Chaetodon miliaris**, *feeds on plankton.*

**137** – *The saddle-shaped blotch distinguishes the saddleback,* **Chaetodon ephippium**. *They are considered to be generalist feeders.*

**138** – *Tolerant of turbid waters,* **Chaetodon octofasciatus** *can easily be found on sediment-stressed reefs.*

**139** – **Chaetodon bennetti** *can be immediately distinguished by the distinct dark patch and the two bright diagonal stripes against a yellow background.*

136 ▲ 137 ▼

115

**140 – Chaetodon lineolatus** *is generally one of the largest butterflyfishes which feeds mainly on soft and hard corals.*

**141 – Heniochus acuminatus** *makes its majestic appearance usually in pairs or in schools. Its colour pattern closely resembles that of the moorish idol,* **Zanclus cornutus**.

**142 – Chaetodon xanthurus** *is a rather uncommon species and seeing it is a rare opportunity.*

**143 – Forcipiger longirostris** *has a long snout that enables it to probe efficiently in tight spaces between the branches of corals.*

140 ▲ 141 ▼

# Damselfishes

Damselfishes form the most abundant group on coral reefs in terms of species and numbers. They are mainly small-sized species without food value. The more colourful species are collected for the aquarium trade.

**144 – Dascyllus aruanus** *can usually be found in large aggregations taking shelter within the branches of hard corals.*

**145 – Chromis** *also forms large aggregations on reefs.*

**146, 147 –** *Clownfishes are colourful and well known for their association with sea anemones. They have a peculiar way of wriggling their bodies amongst the tentacles of their host from which they seldom venture too far. Each species has its distinctive markings as shown by* **Amphiprion ocellaris** *with its three vertical broad bands (right), and* **Amphiprion perideraion**, *a paler but nonetheless distinctive clownfish (below).*

144 ▲

145 ▲ 146 ▼

147

# Parrotfishes and wrasses

Parrotfishes and wrasses may look very similar in body shape and colour pattern but are distinguished from each other by their feeding habits arising from their different dentition. Most parrotfishes (also known as scarids) scrape off live corals in their desire for the coral's algal symbiont. Parrotfishes usually have fused teeth resembling parrot beaks, while wrasses have small separate pointed teeth.

**148** – Many parrotfishes like **Scarus** form a thin mucous bag around themselves at night so that they remain protected while they "sleep".

**149** – The small cleaner wrasse, **Labroides dimidiatus**, serves a cleaning role by feeding on parasites and algae off the bodies of other species of fish. It is seen here cleaning the butterflyfish **Chaetodon kleinii**.

**150** – The checkerboard wrasse, **Halichoeres hortulanus**, is so called because of its distinct pastel patchwork design of black and white.

**151** – **Thalassoma lunare** are active opportunistic scavengers and home in immediately on a food source.

148 ▲ 149 ▼

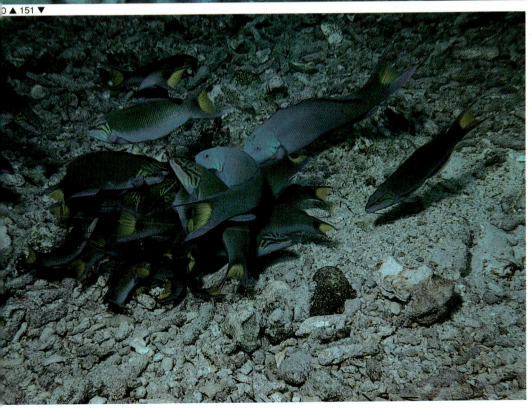

# Triggerfishes and surgeonfishes

*Triggerfishes are mainly associated with coral reefs. When sheltering within crevices, they can erect their dorsal fin spines and pelvic fin spines so that it is almost impossible to dislodge them. Many are specialized feeders of sea urchins. The surgeonfishes are seen in shallow waters where they graze chiefly on algae. Some ingest sand which are excreted after the detrital contents have been digested.*

**152** – *The pinktail triggerfish,* **Melichthys vidua**, *is not commonly seen.*

**153** – *The clown triggerfish,* **Balistoides conspicillum**, *inhabits the outer reef slopes. It has a striking colour pattern.*

**154** – *The dotty triggerfish,* **Balistoides viridescens**, *is another inhabitant of coral reefs.*

**155** – *The colour pattern of* **Acanthurus glaucopareius** *makes it an attractive surgeonfish associated with coral reefs.*

152 ▲ 153 ▼

4 ▲ 155 ▼

## Serranids (basslets and groupers)

Serranids belong to a family which is widely distributed throughout the tropics and subtropics. They include groupers, coral trouts and the smaller basslets. The larger groupers and coral trouts are important food fishes while the basslets are collected for the aquarium trade.

156 – Serranids are usually large carnivorous fish but include small-sized species such as **Anthias mortoni** and **A. tuka**, commonly referred to as basslets.

157 – The red grouper or coral trout, **Cephalopholis miniatus**, lives at relatively deeper depths under rock ledges and corals. The young ones make attractive aquarium fish with their iridescent blue spots against a brillant red background, but adults are more often sought for food.

158 – Boenacki's grouper, **Cephalopholis boenack**, is usually associated with disturbed reefs in sheltered waters.

156 ▲ 157 ▼

158

124

## Snappers and grunts

Snappers, also known as lutjanids, and grunts are popular food fishes because of their good-tasting flesh. Snappers can grow to large sizes and fetch considerable prices. Grunts have large mouths, with one group called the sweetlips because of their thick puckered lips and good taste. It is also common to hear them emit grunting sounds.

**159-161** – *Sweetlips such as the spotted* **P. chaetodontoides**, *the striped* **P. diagrammus** *and the yellow finned* **Plectorhynchus lineatus** *have distinguishable colour markings, but are instantly recognized by their thick lips. All three species are common in the South China Sea.*

**162** – *Snappers such as* **Lutjanus kasmira** *usually form large schools.*

159 ▲ 160 ▼

# Pelagic fishes

Fishes which swim long distances are streamlined and adapted for fast swimming. Almost all of them travel in large schools, some of which number by the thousands.

**163 – Caranx melampygus**, like all jacks, have laterally flattened bodies. The silvery colouration which helps to prevent the casting of shadows below makes them difficult to detect from above or below by both predators and prey.

**164** – The great barrucada, **Sphyraena barracuda**, sometimes hovers motionlessly in the water. A voracious carnivore, it has been reported to attack humans but these attacks are suspected to be unintentional.

**165, 166 – Caesio diagramma**, with black markings on the tail tips, and **C. tile**, with a stripe along each tail fin, swim about in very large schools which increase their chances of survival. Scattering in every direction, they often confuse the predator, but regrouping quickly to continue on their journey.

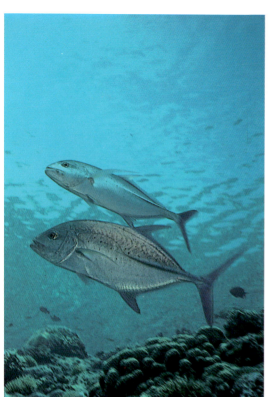

163 ▲ 164 ▼

▲ 166 ▼

129

# Venomous and poisonous fishes

A fair number of fish species is regarded as venomous or poisonous and should be avoided or handled with extreme caution. Venomous fishes have spines which are attached to glands containing toxins. As the spine inflicts the wound, toxins are pumped into the victim. Some toxins are powerful and can cause death. Poisonous fishes have toxins concentrated within specific organs or tissues. These toxins act on the predator or the person consuming the fish.

**167** – The young of the catfish, **Plotosus lineatus**, is usually seen in tightly packed schools on shallow reefs.

**168** – The stonefish, **Scorpaenopsis cirrhosa**, has a shape and colour that allows it to blend in with the surroundings, so that unsuspecting prey can be easily captured as they swim close by.

**169** – Lionfishes such as **Pterois antennata**, with elaborate finnage and seemingly harmless, do possess venomous spines.

**170** – The porcupine fish, **Diodon hystrix**, is related to the puffers but has moveable spines all over the head and body.

167 ▲ 168 ▼

9 ▲ 170 ▼

# Other reef fishes

Fish species diversity is high in the South China Sea. They exhibit a wide range of adaptive strategies which enable them to exploit the many different niches found in the sea. The variation in shape, structure and behaviour makes them interesting to observe.

**171** – Hawkfishes like **Paracirrhites fosteri** are small bottom inhabitants of reefs, often seen perched on hard corals, soft corals and gorgonians. They have free projecting rays on the lower part of the pectoral fins which enable this perching habit.

**172** – The threadfin bream, **Scolopsis bilineatus**, is distinguished by a curved white stripe that stretches from the mouth to the dorsal fin.

**173** – **Aeoliscus strigatus**, commonly known as razorfish, has a peculiar body shape that allows it to swim vertically and hover between the spines of sea urchins.

171 ▲ 172 ▼

173

174 ▲

175 ▲ 176 ▼

**174, 177** – *One species of trumpetfish,* **Aulostomus chinensis**, *occurs in this area. It can reach a length of 50cm. Two colour variations of this odd-shaped fish can be seen, dark greenish-brown with pale stripes or bright yellow.*

**175** – *The anglerfish,* **Antennarius**, *is a master fisherman which depends on effective camouflage. Its first dorsal spine is modified to look like a bait which it uses to entice prey towards its mouth.*

**176** – *Another species of razorfish,* **Centriscus scutatus**, *is distinguished by its silvery-yellow and almost transparent colouration. They move in schools around coastal waters.*

177

178 ▲

179 ▲ 180 ▼

**178** – *Sub-adults of the batfish,* **Platax orbicularis***, have a deep, almost circular body, with distinctly extended dorsal and anal fins. The species shows an interesting continuous change in body and fin shape as it grows.*

**179** – *The variegated lizardfish,* **Synodus variegatus***, is often seen in sand-rubble areas of the reef. Lizardfishes have depressed heads like that of a lizard and elongated cylindrical bodies.*

**180, 181** – *Cardinalfishes such as* **Apogon aureus** *with their orange belly and electric blue head markings, and the less colourful* **Sphaeramia nematoptera** *are nocturnal, and hide in caves and crevices during the day.*

181

182 ▲

**182** – *The squirrelfish,* **Myripristis adustus,** *is also nocturnal and spends most of the day sheltering in caves or under ledges.*

**183** – *The emperor angelfish,* **Pomacanthus imperator,** *is easily one of the most striking of the angelfish family.*

**184** – *Like most squirrelfishes,* **Myripristis vittatus** *has a generally reddish hue.*

**185** – **Sargocentron spinifer,** *also a squirrelfish, has yellow pectoral, pelvic and anal fins.*

183 ▲ 184 ▼

185 ▶

186 ▲

# Reptiles

*Turtles and sea snakes are among the reptiles that have returned to live in the sea. Being air breathers, they must surface for air but are adapted to remain underwater for long periods with each breath.*

**186** – *The green turtle,* **Chelonia mydas**, *uses its flippers to push sand over the nest to conceal its eggs. Within two months, the hatchlings will emerge from the nest and instinctively head for the sea. This is when the hatchlings are most vulnerable to predators.*

**187, 189** – *Sea snakes such as* **Hydrophis** *all have their tails laterally flattened like an oar for effective propulsion in the water. It is common to find aggregations of them.*

**188** – *The amphibious sea snake,* **Laticauda colubrina**, *is commonly found around small islands. They breed on shore and are the only sea snakes that lay eggs.*

187 ▲ 188 ▼

189 ▶

# INDEX

**A**

*Acalcygorgia* 60, 62
*Acanthaster planci* 92, 94
*Acanthurus glaucopareius* 122
*Acrometoides purpureus* 30, 66
*Acropora hyacinthus* 46
*Acropora nobilis* 46
*Acropora splendida* 46
*Actinopyga lecanora* 98
*Adamsia* 22
*Aeoliscus strigatus* 132
*Aetobatus narinari* 110
*Aglaophenia* 64
*Amphiprion ocellaris* 56, 118
*Amphiprion perideraion* 118
*Antennarius* 134
*Anthias mortoni* 124
*Antipathes* 68
*Apogon aureus* 136
*Asthenosoma intermedium* 104
*Atrina* 76
*A. tuka* 124
*Aulostomus chinensis* 134

**B**

*Balistoides conspicillum* 122
*Balistoides viridescens* 122
*Bohadschia argus* 100
*Bohadschia graffei* 98
*Briareum stechei* 22

**C**

*Caesio diagramma* 128
*Calpurnus verrucosa* 78
*Carangoides* 36
*Caranx melampygus* 128
*Carcharhinus albimarginatus* 110
*Casella atromarginata* 84
*Casella cincta* 84
*Caulerpa* 40
*Centriscus scutatus* 134
*Cephalopholis* 37
*Cephalopholis boenack* 124
*Cephalopholis miniatus* 124
*Chaetodon bennetti* 114
*Chaetodon ephippium* 114
*Chaetodon kleinii* 120
*Chaetodon lineolatus* 116
*Chaetodon xanthurus* 116
*Chaetodon miliaris* 114
*Chaetodon octofasciatus* 114
*Charonia tritonis* 80
*Chelonia mydas* 140
*Choriaster granulatus* 94

*Chromis* 118
*Chromodoris* 84
*Chromodoris coi* 86
*Cirrhipathes* 68
*Cirrhipathes anguina* 29
*Clathrina* 42
*Clavelina* 108
*Comanthus bennetti* 106
*Comatula* 106
*Conus aulicus* 78
*Ctenocella* 62
*C. tile* 128
*Culcita novaeguineae* 94
*Cypraea tigris* 78

**D**

*Dascyllus aruanus* 118
*Dendrophyllia* 44
*Dendronephthya* 54
*Diadema setosum* 102
*Diodon hystrix* 130
*Distichopora violacea* 64
*Dromia dormia* 88

**E**

*Echinometra mathaei* 104
*Echinothrix calamaris* 104
*Efflatounaria* 52
*Elisella* 58
*Epinephalus* 9, 37
*Euplexaura* 62

**F**

*Flabellina* 82
*Flabellina rubrolineata* 84
*Forcipiger longirostris* 116
*Fromia monilis* 94
*Fungia* 25

**G**

*Goniopora* 46
*Gymnothorax* 112

**H**

*Halichoeres hortulanus* 120
*Heniochus acuminatus* 116
*Heterocentrotus mammillatus* 102
*Himerometra* 18
*Holothuria edulis* 100
*Hydrophis* 140

**I**
*Isis 60*

**J**
*Juncella 58*

**L**
*Lamprometra 106*
*Laticauda colubrina 140*
*Leptoria phrygia 22*
*Linckia laevigata 92*
*Lithothamnion 40*
*Lobophytum 54*
*Lutjanus kasmira 126*

**M**
*Macropipus 90*
*Melichthys vidua 122*
*Melithaea 58*
*Millepora 64*
*Mycedium elephantotus 50*
*Myripristis adustus 138*
*Myripristis vittatus 138*

**N**
*Nembrotha 86*

**O**
*Ophiolepis superba 96*
*Ophiomastix 96*
*Ophiothrix 96*
*Ovula ovum 52, 78*

**P**
*Pachyseris 48*
*Paracirrhites fosteri 132*
*Parerythropodium fulvum fulvum 54*
*Pavona cactus 48*
*P. chaetodontoides 126*
*P. diagrammus 126*
*Pectinia alcicornis 48*
*Pedum spondyloideum 76*
*Periclimenes 90*
*Phyllidia ocellata 86*
*Phyllidia varicosa 86*
*Phyllodesmium 82*
*Phyllophorus 100*
*Phyllorhiza punctata 66*
*Platax orbicularis 136*
*Plectorhynchus lineatus 126*
*Plerogya sinuosa 44*
*Plotosus lineatus 130*
*Polycarpa aurata 108*
*Pomacanthus imperator 138*

*Porites 46, 72, 76*
*Pseudoceros affinis 70*
*Pteraeolidia semperi 82*
*Pterois antennata 130*
*Pycnodonte 76*

**R**
*Radianthus 56*
*Radianthus ritteri 56*

**S**
*Sabella 72*
*Sabellastarte 72*
*Sarcophyton 52*
*Sargassum 40*
*Sargocentron spinifer 138*
*Scarus 120*
*Scolopsis bilineatus 132*
*Scorpaenopsis cirrhosa 130*
*Sepia 80*
*Seriatopora hystrix 50*
*Solenocaulen 62*
*Sphaeramia nematoptera 136*
*Sphyraena barracuda 128*
*Spirobranchus giganteus 72*
*Stenopus hispidus 90*
*Stichopus chloronotus 100*
*Strombus 80*
*Sula sula 14*
*Symphyllia 50*
*Synapta masculata 98*
*Synodus variegatus 136*

**T**
*Taeniura lymna 110*
*Thalamita 88*
*Thalassoma lunare 120*
*Thysanozoon flavomaculatum 70*
*Toxopneustes pileolus 102*
*Triaenodon obesus 110*
*Tridacna 26*
*Tridacna maxima 74*
*Tubastrea aurea 44*
*Turbinaria 48*

**V**
*Valonia 40*

**X**
*Xenia 54*
*Xestospongia 42*

**Z**
*Zanclus cornutus 116*

## Suggested Readings

Chou, L.M. 1988. *A Guide to the Coral Reef Life of Singapore.* Singapore: Singapore Science Centre. 128 pp.

George, D. and George, J. 1979. *Marine Life: An Illustrated Encyclopedia of Invertebrates in the Sea.* London: Lionel Leventhal Ltd. 288 pp.

Henrey, L. 1982. *Coral Reefs of Malaysia and Singapore.* Kuala Lumpur: Longman Malaysia Sdn. Bhd. 81 pp.

Smith, M.M. and Heemstra, P.C. 1986. *Smiths' Sea Fishes.* Berlin: Springer-Verlag. 1047 pp.

Veron, J.E.N. 1986. *Corals of Australia and the Indo-Pacific.* Australia: Angus and Robertson. 644 pp.

White, A. 1987. *Philippine Coral Reefs: A Natural History Guide.* Philippines: New Day Publishers. 223 pp.

## Photo Credits

**Porfirio M. Alino,** 23 (bottom), 50 (No. 20), 52 (Nos. 22, 23), 54 (No. 26), 73 (No. 61)

**Juny Binamira,** 127 (No. 162)

**Carl J. Ferraris,** 35, 61 (No. 38), 118 (No. 145)

**Gretchen Hutchinson,** 67 (No. 50), 80 (Nos. 72, 73), 110-111 (Nos. 128, 131), 123 (No. 154), 128 (No. 163), 139 (No. 185)

**A. Michael Jones,** 23 (top), 26 (bottom), 31, 33, 42 (No. 5), 44 (No. 9), 45 (No. 10), 53 (No. 24), 56 (No. 30), 58 (No. 33), 60 (No. 36), 62 (No. 40), 65 (No. 46), 68 (No. 51), 72 (Nos. 58, 59), 78 (No. 70), 81 (Nos. 74, 75), 82-83 (Nos. 77, 78), 84 (Nos. 80, 81), 86 (Nos. 83, 84), 90-91 (Nos. 90, 92, 93), 92 (No. 94), 95 (No. 100), 96-97 (Nos. 101, 102, 103, 104), 102 (No. 115), 104-105 (Nos. 118, 119), 108-109 (Nos. 124, 125, 126, 127), 118 (No. 146), 129 (No. 166), 130-131 (Nos. 167, 168, 170), 132-133 (Nos. 172, 173), 134-135 (Nos. 175, 177), 136 (No. 180)

**Khoo Soo Seng,** cover, 6, 11, 18, 30, 36, 46 (No. 11), 55 (No. 28), 62 (No. 41), 66 (No. 47), 68 (No. 52), 84 (No. 79), 98 (Nos. 105, 106), 100 (No. 111), 110 (No. 129), 113 (No. 135), 117 (No. 143), 127 (No. 161), 128-129 (Nos. 164, 165)

**Clive Lightfoot,** 111 (No. 130), 136 (No. 178)

Michael Loh, cover inset

**Teodulo F. Luchavez,** 46 (No. 13), 64 (No. 44)

**John W. McManus,** 15 (bottom), 24, 27 (top), 47 (No. 14), 50 (No. 19), 106 (No. 121), 119 (No. 147), 120 (No. 149), 126 (No. 160), 134 (No. 176)

**Ramon I. Miclat,** 26 (top), 54 (No. 27), 86 (No. 85), 94 (No. 97), 131 (No. 169)

**Reef Ecology Study Team, National University of Singapore,** 8, 12, 15 (top), 16, 19, 20, 40-41 (Nos. 1, 2, 3, 4), 43 (No. 7), 44 (No. 8), 48-49 (Nos. 15, 16, 17, 18), 51 (No. 21), 54 (No. 25), 56 (No. 29), 57 (No. 31), 59 (No. 35), 63 (No. 42), 64 (No. 43), 64 (No. 45), 66 (No. 48), 70-71 (Nos. 56, 57), 73 (No. 60), 74-75 (Nos. 62, 63, 64), 76-77 (Nos. 65, 66, 67), 78 (Nos. 68, 69), 82 (No. 76), 85 (No. 82), 87 (No. 86), 89 (No. 89), 93 (No. 96), 94 (Nos. 98, 99), 98-99 (Nos. 107, 108), 100-101 (Nos. 109, 110, 112), 102 (Nos. 113, 114), 103 (No. 116), 104-105 (Nos. 117, 120), 106-107 (Nos. 122, 123), 112 (No. 132), 115 (No. 138), 117 (No. 142), 121 (No. 151), 125 (No. 158), 137 (No. 181), 140 (No. 186)

**Michael Ross,** 37, 46 (No. 12), 92 (No. 95), 118 (No. 144), 132 (No. 171)

**Robert G. Sellers,** 38, 114-115 (Nos. 137, 139), 138 (No. 183)

**Alan T. White,** 14, 22, 27 (bottom), 28, 34, 42 (No. 6), 57 (No. 32), 58 (No. 34), 60 (No. 37), 62 (No. 39), 66 (No. 49), 69 (Nos. 53, 54), 70 (No. 55), 79 (No. 71), 88 (Nos. 87, 88), 90 (No. 91), 112-113 (Nos. 133, 134), 114 (No. 136), 116 (Nos. 140, 141), 117 (No. 142), 120-121 (Nos. 148, 150), 122-123 (Nos. 152, 153, 155), 124 (Nos. 156, 157), 126 (No. 159), 134 (No. 174), 136 (No. 179), 138 (Nos. 182, 184), 140-141 (Nos. 187, 188, 189)

.......................................................

## Scientific Editor: Edgardo D. Gomez